Mason Jar Gifts.

The Ultimate Guide for Making Amazing DIY Mason Jar Gifts

Catherine Dorsey Copyright © 2015

All rights reserved. No part of this book may be reproduced in any form without permission in writing from the author. Reviewers may quote brief passages in reviews.

Disclaimer

No part of this publication may be reproduced or transmitted in any form or by any means, mechanical or electronic, including photocopying or recording, or by any information storage and retrieval system, or transmitted by email without permission in writing from the publisher.

While all attempts and efforts have been made to verify the information held within this publication, neither the author nor the publisher assumes any responsibility for errors, omissions, or opposing interpretations of the content herein.

This book is for entertainment purposes only. The views expressed are those of the author alone, and should not be taken as expert instruction or commands. The reader of this book is responsible for his or her own actions when it comes to reading the book.

Adherence to all applicable laws and regulations, including international, federal, state, and local governing professional licensing, business practices, advertising, and all other aspects of doing business in the US, Canada, or any other jurisdiction is the sole responsibility of the purchaser or reader.

Neither the author nor the publisher assumes any responsibility or liability whatsoever on the behalf of the purchaser or reader of these materials.

Any received slight of any individual or organization is purely unintentional.

Table of Contents

Introduction

Chapter 1 - The Many Benefits of Mason Jar Gifts

Chapter 2- Gift Recommendations

Chapter 3- Deciding on the Perfect Gift

Chapter 4- Seasonal Gifting

Chapter 5- Share and Celebrate!

Chapter 6 - Uses for Mason Jar Gifts Afterwards

Conclusion

Bonus: Gifts in Jars you could Easily Make

Introduction

I want to thank you and congratulate you for downloading this book, Mason Jar Gifts: The Gifts the Keep Giving. This book contains proven steps and strategies for enhancing the joy of the holiday or birthday party of your loved one through choice of the perfect gift. In addition, this book provides cheap and easy recommendations which can make this dream come true, personalizing your gift to show the receiver of it just how much you truly care.

If you take the time to read this book fully and apply the information held within this book will help you to understand the many creative possibilities of gift giving Mason jars provide. If your family is anything like mine, you go through jam and jelly pretty fast, and thus probably have some jars just lying in the pantry. Why not put them to good use? Peruse through the information in this book, which was written to entertain as well as educate, and learn just how you can spice up your holidays with a Mason jar gift.

This book continues as follows. It consists of six chapters. The first chapter discusses the many benefits of Mason jar gifting. The second chapter makes recommendations for Mason jar gifts. The third chapter covers how to decide on the perfect thing to put in your Mason jar gift. In the fourth chapter I talk about how these gifts can be made and given depending on the holiday or special occasion. The fifth chapter addresses sharing and celebrating Mason jar gifts with your family. The sixth chapter covers all the great things you can do with your jars if their contents have outlived their usefulness. Finally, the last section concludes.

At the end you'll be an expert on Mason jar gifting, and one of the best gift givers around. They say that it's better to give than to receive. I can't say with full certainty that I'd want to give away such a well-suited present. When I see the look on my partner's or my best friend's face when he sees it however it all becomes worth it. Thanks again for downloading this book, I hope you enjoy it!

Chapter 1
The Many Benefits of Mason Jar Gifts

There are so many benefits of giving Mason jar gifts that it's hard for a writer to know where to begin. This section outlines some of the reasons in the attempt of spreading the joy of the Mason jar gift as a preferable option.

First of all, Mason jar gifts are very practical. They're inexpensive themselves, and often recycled from their use as a container of food or condiments in the house. Yet they carry a strange stylistic effect of being appropriate for gifting despite this high functionality and prior usage. This is essentially the best of both worlds. In these tough economic times, it's really important to have something that is thrifty without compromising the quality of the gift. Mason jars are just such a gift, also because they can be doubly used for practical purposes by the receiver after already serving great purpose to anyone who has owned them in the past.

The second great benefit of this gift type is the versatility of the options for what can go inside it. More ideas are given with respect to this in the second section. But essentially, anything that can fit inside the jar can be given, as well as a nearly unlimited combination of small gifts that can be enjoyed one by one. This also means that the gift can be intensely personalized, and well-catered to the individual. It's considered a great sign of respect and informs the closeness of a relationship when a person can choose the perfect gift, because this often requires a lot of knowledge about what he or she is interested in. Lots of small gifts can be the perfect formula, or rather if the receiver loves all of one thing that much more, maybe that's a sign for the giver to keep things simple.

These days' practical gifts are often preferred to extravagant ones. Also it can be unreasonable to expect someone to reciprocate when given a really expensive gift. Instead, give them something they can use practically around the house and they'll be grateful. One doesn't always need to have diamond encrusted earrings when more practical needs must be met.

While a Mason jar gift can be (very) inexpensive if that is the desire, keep in mind that great things come in small packages as well. Moreover, a Mason jar can be the perfect place to conceal something of great value, like jewelry. The effect of this on the receiver can be even higher, because generally one does not expect to receive a gift of such import in a Mason jar. Engagement rings too might be an excellent option!

If you're interested in more specific options for gifts and the methods used to make them, check out the next chapter, which provides 30 different gift ideas for those that need a push in the right direction. In later chapters I discuss how you might best match up your gift depending on the person.

Chapter 2: Gift Recommendations

This chapter discusses many of the wondrous options for Mason jar gifts. Brief and easy descriptions are provided to make them, whereas some of these can be store-bought. Of course a special sentiment is always expressed when more effort is put into the gift, especially when you decide to go to the trouble of making the contents and decorating the gift yourself. Design and gift ideas vary. Some of them are for practical usage in the household. Others provide aesthetic improvement. Some are simply good to eat. Everyone likes to have delectable food items around. Take a look below to discover new gift ideas in these 30 recommendations.

1. Poured Candles

Either buy a jar with a pre-made candle or heat and pour your own wax. Be sure to leave the wick intact and sticking out. These are available in a variety of aromas that will add to the holiday atmosphere.

2. Candy!

This is the simplest gift ever. Fill the jar with candy that your loved one likes most. The perfect jar decoration for this gift is a soft paper exterior held together with a rubber-band near the cap.

3. Canned Goods

Peaches, apples or pears are always great to have in a canned, especially during the winter-time when they're out of season. You're bound to have cravings. Less than extravagant, this is a practical gift that is appropriate for everyone.

4. Herbs and Spices

Let the jar be a dispenser for your loved one's favorite herbs and spices. This may require a set of jars, perhaps smaller ones. Lots of families make a point of collecting spices over the years. Share with them a special spice that's used in ethnic food that they haven't tried before. This way you can help them expand their horizons as well.

5. Soap Dispenser

Drill a half-inch hold in the lid and screw on a dispenser pump that you can purchase at a local arts and crafts store. Also, these are available to purchase pre-made. Add whatever soap you want and help to save the world by avoiding excessive usage of plastic.

6. Sewing Kit

A key for winter warmth, sowing enthusiasts will love a quaint way to store their materials, and will think of you every time they need to take them out again. This may even make them a bit more likely to sow you your own new set of hat and mittens!

7. Twine Dispenser

How about this for practicality! Put your rolls of twine inside, and all you need is a small hole drilled in the lid. You can even stack them and have various threads coming out, so you'll only need one jar to dispense all of your twines.

8. Salt and Pepper Shaker

Spice up your dinner with salt and pepper shaker jars. These too come pre-made or can be made based on your preferences. Some people are satisfied with ordinary salt and pepper, but the connoisseur may require a subtler taste!

9. Light Display

Drilling holes in the sides of the lid allows you to string up your jars. Putting lights in them creates a special kind of effect, a nice ambiance for the porch. Light up your friends and relatives holidays by giving them a lighted Mason jar gift set.

10.   Bathroom Accessory Holder

Mount those babies on the wall and you can put your toothbrush and other morning implements in them. You might even think ahead of time to fill the jar with a set of special toiletries, one of the most practical gifts ever!

11.   Photo Frame

Put old photos of you with your friends or family in the jar, so they can remember the times that you've had together. The slimness of this gift will leave the rest of the jar open to special surprises, including other little trinkets to celebrate and remember your past.

12. Speaker

Check this out. You can purchase Mason jars that have been converted into external speakers. This is like a cross between a stereo upgrade and the perfect gift for grandma. Your music will sound better coming from Mason jar speakers.

13. Liquid Dispenser

Give your family or friends a Mason jar that's got a tap built into it so that they can fill it with whatever liquid their heart desires. This would be a wonderful little alternative to a family pitcher at the dinner table, and certainly adds character to the set.

14. Cooking Implement Holder

How about filling up an oversized jar with cooking tools? The implements will probably need to be sticking out from the jar, so this present is probably best wrapped and filled in bubble wrap as well to conceal the cooking goodness and to protect the integrity of the glassware as well.

15. Cookie Dough

If you want to give away a special treat, fill up the jar with a rare and special kind of cookie dough. This gives the receiver the homework of doing a bit of baking, but the aroma and the taste of the cookies will remind your friends of you. Try wrapping the lid up in a little bow that matches the color theme of the evening.

16. Layered Salad

This one obviously can't be kept under the Christmas tree for any extended length of time, but it allows for a special surprise in the short time. Take it with you to picnics. Salad on the bottom, then carrots, radishes and tomatoes are added, and finally, salad dressing on top. Mix it all up and enjoy yourself in the park.

17. Past Letters and Correspondence

If there's someone you have a close relationship with, perhaps a spouse or a significant other, and you want to reconnect with them, copy down your past correspondence on nice sheets of paper and include them. Also put in there some blank sheets of paper and a nice pen to give that special person the incentive to continue writing you in the future.

18. Cupcakes

Bake up a storm with cupcake molds that are shaped like your Mason jar glass. When finished simply be careful in taking them out and putting them in the Mason jar glass. What are the holidays without ample sweets?

19. Birthday Gifts for Kids

Fill up a Mason jar with assorted colorful birthday materials. Balloons, chocolate medallions, paper hats and mini toys are a great way to show that you care. This is the perfect mini birthday kit.

20. Flowers

Go out to your garden or to the flower shop and pick out something that will brighten your spouse's day. Flowers are a classic way to show that you care, and while the flowers themselves will wilt, the jar will remain a useful gift.

21. Coffee

Nothing makes the coffee drinker happier than getting surprise exposure to new kinds of Arabica coffee. Fill the jar with one kind of coffee or an assortment. The receiver of this gift will have to thank you endlessly for helping him or her wake up early in the morning.

22. Tea

Assorted teas can be as great to drink as coffee, especially late at night when one doesn't want to be kept up all night by caffeine. There are all sorts of teas around the world. How about some mint leaves too? It only takes five minutes of soaking to completely change the taste.

23. Hot Chocolate

Had enough drink ideas? If you haven't considered making a gift of hot chocolate it's time to get with the program. This is a perfect gift for when it's cold outside and adds comfort to the winter of even the worst scrooge.

24. Mason Jar Lamp

Get a lamp that can be mounted on the wall or stands alone. These will add character to the bedroom or living room. Best store-bought unless you've got some carpentry skills, these make for the perfect lighting implement.

25. Oil Lamps

Fill a jar up with oil and set the wick atop alight! Many of these jars come with aesthetic contents that make the jar look easier on the eyes. This is a longer lasting alternative to candles, and also is great for the environmentalist as it takes you off the grid.

26. Quick Bread

Include nuts, gingerbread and chocolate chips for a delectable mix of goodness that everyone will enjoy.

27. Glowstick Jar

Empty the contents of a glowstick into your jar, and add diamond glitter to the mix. This is the perfect gift for a young princess. Be cautious in making this as the materials can be harmful

28. Wineglass

Believe it or not, there's a special kind of Mason jar that's a play on wineglasses. These are store-bought, and perfect to pull out when you're looking for a twist in a romantic evening.

29. Pasta

Nothing spells home like pasta with all the herbs and spices included. Far better than a box of noodles, include seashell pasta pieces so they'll fit.

30. Salsa

These jars are perfect if you want to have some salsa and chips in a sports gathering. Create your own concoction rather than relying on the store bought stuff.

Chapter 3: Deciding on the Perfect Gift

If you like the idea of giving a Mason jar gift but are not quite sure in exactly what form to give it to your loved one or co-worker, take a look below for lots of options. Gifts are always more interesting when they're personalized, and different types of people like all sorts of things. Of course, the type of gift you give should also depend heavily on your relationship with the person in question, ranging from the informal to the intimate, and the familial to the professional. Don't worry though; there is an appropriate gift for everyone.

Co-Worker

Gifts in these circles are usually characterized by fun little trinkets or gags that try to mock the over-serious tone that gets taken on in some of our workplaces these days. Quite often, gift exchanges are carried out during the holidays, meaning that you may not need to worry much about the contents of the gift at all, especially if it's going to be selected by a co-worker randomly. We all love having secret Santas. Office-related implements are great, a new stapler, for instance, to replace the one that your co-workers have been wrestling over all year. Just remember though that a workplace gift is a workplace gift. If you want to give something intimate to one of your co-workers, it may best be done in private.

Friend

Depending on how well you know each other, you might be able to go all out with a gift for your friend. You probably know what he's been wanting all this time better than anyone, so go for it if you're feeling particularly generous. Good friends often enjoy throwbacks to when they were kids, electronics, and hobby-related gifts. We all need a pair of socks every now and then, but that's where you grandparents come in. Friends are supposed to buy each other gifts that are exciting.

Parents

Parents are generally happy that you remembered to buy them something, and you should, as a small token of appreciation for all the stuff they've put up with over the years! Your parents may already be worried about accumulating too many random trinkets that they'll have to find a place to put around the house, so think practical when it comes to the parents. Cater to your mother's feminine side by getting her candles. Flowers can also be hugely meaningful. Your father might be glad to get some tools, although not the same ones that he got last year!

Siblings

If your brother or sister has just had children, s/he may want something that can help with the baby. A cute light display would be wonderful. Otherwise, how about something relating to their interests? You are sure to know them about as well as anyone.

Significant Other

Now things are getting intimate. If you're what you would consider a serious couple you may want to step it up with the gifts. These could somehow inform your special relationship. Unplanned gifts can make his or her days unpredictable in a wonderful way. Clearly this is one of the few relationships where it might be appropriate to introduce some spice into things.

Spouse

Now that you're married, you can think of gifts as more practically things that might work well around the house. Be careful in presenting something however as a gift that you both might need. A special kind of food or drink in a jar may do the trick, or another option is to hide that small valuable gift in a Mason jar, making it that much more of a surprise.

Grandmother

Last but not least, don't think that your grandmother won't enjoy a Mason jar gift as well. In fact, she may be able to reminisce about the times when these were how general stores used to stock their goods on the shelves! Now, that is certainly cause for nostalgia. So what is the perfect gift for grandmother. This may be difficult considering that she's accumulated so much stuff over the course of her life. This may be a valuable clue though. Grandmothers often have collections, and are glad to expand them, although in the end it's the thought that counts.

Grandfather

If you can distract your grandmother for long enough, you can justify getting grandpa a jar of whisky without getting him into trouble. Otherwise you may have to choose something more suitable to the tenor of an amiable evening with the family. Grandpa might like some nails for his workshop so he can get out of the house or maybe even a special kind of sweets.

Chapter 4: Seasonal Gifting

When it comes to maintaining relationships, the best way to show that you care is to make a real effort when the holidays roll around, and get creative in your holiday themed gift ideas. Consider the symbolism behind a gift, and remember that giving is always better than receiving. Mason jar gifts allow you to spread the love around cheaply. Way better than getting nothing, get a person in your life a little something. In may not seem like much, but a little goes a long way. That small sentiment could really make someone's day.

Often, having those extra presents around on a birthday just makes the event seem grander. At Christmas, too, you don't want one small gift under the tree, even if it's a great one, what you really want is an overflowing of presents so grand that people can hardly walk in that part of the room. This doesn't require giant expenditures but it does require some forethought. Also remember that there are all sorts of holidays throughout the year. This chapter takes a look at how you can celebrate the holidays with different Mason jar gift ideas.

The first are the most obvious. Holidays like Christmas host times in which jars are gifted, often with a visual theme to match. These express the Christmas spirit faithfully. There's no reason not to give out Mason jars on Hanukah as well. They can be filled with dreidels as well as anything else. Mother's day and Father's day are a great time to show your appreciation to your parents, and let's not forget your grandparents too, even if there isn't a designated day for them. Valentine's Day is a must for lovers, and the perfect time for men and women to say that secret nothing that they've been meaning to utter for months. Wedding anniversaries must always be remembered by husbands, and are a wonderful way for married couples to celebrate the years they've spent together. Shorter term couples may also enjoy their one-month anniversary, though this may only be the beginning of a great relationship!

Saint Patrick's Day is perhaps the most appropriate holiday during which to gift a Mason jar filled with booze. Just make sure you don't give the same person too many or he may get too drunk and fall into the Chicago River by accident! Halloween on the other hand is quite clearly perfect for spookily themed gifts of candy. Dress it up as a ghost and place them around the house afterwards to add to the scary atmosphere or take the empty jug and fill it with spooky lights. There is virtually no end to the themed gifts you can give during the holidays.

You probably wouldn't want to fill a Mason jar with turkey, but on Thanksgiving candy corn is a suitable gift. After all, thanksgiving was all about gift giving, not just stuffing your face until it's completely full! Share that wondrous candy corn! One might not know what to give on a leap year, but it's certainly a rare occasion. Make something up to celebrate this too! Weddings are beautiful occasions, and also a time of gift exchange. The groom could certainly use a couple of cigars to celebrate, and the bride will need a new garter to replace the one she's tossed. On birthdays you've got to take the individual into account, but it should clearly be something that caters to a particular taste. Don't forget what the receiver likes! And remember that above all, it's the thought that counts.

There are other times when people celebrate special events in their lives. High school and university graduation are two big ones. These days computers are a popular gift for high school graduates, but remember, a smart phone may fit within a jar as well. University graduation is an important time too and should be celebrated comparably. After this, a person must go out into the world and transition from being primarily a receiver of Mason jars to a giver of them. This can be a difficult thing to get used to, but with the information here at hand, it should be no problem at all! And how about Bar and Bat Mitzvahs? All the children of the world deserve Mason jar glasses.

Chapter 5: Share and Celebrate!

Our first recommendation in this chapter is to make one of the jars that you give to someone else as a present to someone else as well. Honestly, you would do this for your kids if you had to go out and buy a birthday present for them to give to a friend of theirs. Now it's time to enjoy the spoils of your own generosity. One for them, one for you, that's how the system should work, and this way everybody is happy. Share the joy of these presents with everyone. Holidays aren't the only time to give presents. Sometimes giving presents when they are unexpected is when they are appreciated most.

Celebration is about getting together and sharing your presents as well. The beauty of giving spices away in a Mason jar is that the family will taste them in their food for months to come. It might even become a staple, and fundamentally change their family's recipe. This sort of impact explains why it can be so rewarding to watch the positive impact that you have on people's lives. Mason jars make this a possibility like few other gifts can, especially due to how versatile they can be.

Imagine how fun it would be to sit across the room from one another on the warm and cozy carpeting in your living room with the fireplace ablaze, sharing your gifts with everyone. And afterwards the jars get placed on the mantle above the fireplace for all to see. In a way, they're similar to the surprises in one's stockings. Mason jars are the little wonderful unexpected gift that serves the holidays like an appetizer serves a meal, whetting one's appetite for the real big presents which are to come. Without that little preparation, opening a giant present is too abrupt. Five minutes, and the experience is over. No! This is not how it should be. Unwrapping gifts is meant to be a long and arduous process, at times exhausting. The more gifts you give the more exhausted you are when they are finally opened. But this is a wondrous kind of exhaustion that means you did your best in preparing to take care of your loved ones.

This is a process that nearly all grandparents are familiar with, and they love to shower their children, and mostly their grandchildren with gifts. Grandparents, aunts and uncles have the great gift of being able to spoil their grandkids, nieces and nephews, simply because they aren't around them all that often. Older folks also have the benefit of probably having a lot more Mason jars around than their younger counterparts. Why not take advantage of this?

Chapter 6: Uses for Mason Jar Gifts Afterwards

If you've been given a Mason jar gift and are not 100% sure with what to do with the jar afterwards, here are some ideas. You can get some use out of it around the house in an inventive way. The interesting thing about these jars is that despite their original intention as gifts they seem to look appropriate in just about any of their possible functions, adding a stylistic feel to the house that can be quaint and surprisingly charming. There is a comfort and a pleasure to be found in the many clever ways one can turn an ordinary jar into an appropriate trinket to enrich the cultural and visual atmosphere of your home.

The first and most obvious use for your Mason jar gifts is to hold on to them as a remembrance of the experience of receiving them. Gifts represent the kindness of the gift giver, and his desire to see the receiver express joy in the instance that it's received, and hopefully these positive emotions are maintained throughout the course of any relationship. Sometimes it is easier to connect with that warm feeling of having been cared for through the act of gift giving by having these remembrances around.

Despite how great they might make you feel some people simply don't have the room to collect dozens of empty jars on their mantle. Thankfully, Mason jars are one of the few gifts that it seems are totally appropriate to re-gift. If you've got one too many, don't feel bad about filling them up with some candy (or brandy) and gifting them off to a friend. They'll be grateful for either, and generally will not even be able to tell the difference between this jar and another.

If you'd like to keep the jar but find another use for it, here are some ideas. Mason jars make for great candle holders. Fill them up with water and set alight a floating candle, providing a special romantic ambiance that's even more significant because of your contribution of creativity to the mood of the room. Or, try simply using the jar as a mug for drinks. Some of the classiest venues prefer to use jars for their cocktails. There's a funny kind of irony in this in that jars are used for storing. Since the container is generally bigger than one serving, drinking from a Mason jar sort of feels like tapping liquid straight from the source – it makes your drink look deceptively large, which may be a welcome plus during trying holiday season. Parents will find these especially useful as their glasses will get broken more often, so the replenishing of any kind of glass will be a relief.

Gardeners will find that Mason jars make the perfect tiny little garden patches to put around the house. The glass gives a wonderful cross-section view of the roots, so you can see your plant's progress both above and below ground, making sure that it has plenty of water. Small herbal plants are a great choice for your indoor garden. This keeps them conveniently accessible when you need them for cooking, as well as nearby so that it is more difficult to forget to water them.

If you want to get really inventive, drill a hole in the lid and make your Mason jar into a soap dispenser. It will add so much more character to the room than would an ordinary plastic bottle of branded soap. It also really personalizes your bathroom and makes it your own. It is little trinkets like this that make one feel comfortable at home. This same strategy can also be used to make them in condiment jars. Instead of using cheesy plastic bottles, customize your home dining experience by adding something of your own character to it. For the perpetual snack-eater, a jar is the quintessential holder of all sorts of goodness. Cookies, mints, M&Ms, and skittles are all very much at home in a Mason jar. They keep you stocked up on sugar while you're sitting, reading in your living room, and provide guests with a nice little touch of refreshment with little effort on your part.

Conclusion

Thank you again for downloading this eBook!

I hope this book was able to help you to learn about using Mason jar gifts to show your friends and loved ones how much you care, and that you always know exactly the right gift to give. The next step is to put this information into action and get started in devising your Mason jar gift ideas. The guide above hopefully was of great help in figuring that out.

Just to reiterate, the chapters were as follows. Chapter 1 explained the many different benefits of getting a Mason jar gift. They're cheap, easy, practical and have many uses. Chapter 2 went through a long list of gift ideas and combinations. This should be of help if you're stuck and not exactly sure what to get. Chapter 3 gave a number of specific recommendations for Mason jar gifts, along with a basic guide for how to make or get them. Chapter 4 discussed how to think of the perfect Mason jar gift for the different people in your life. So much variety! Chapter 5 talked about the warm celebrations that you'll enjoy with your family over the years, as well as the joy of both giving and receiving Mason jar gifts. Last but not least, Chapter 6 discussed what you can do with your Mason jar gifts when the presents inside them are all said and done. Plenty of options are available.

This chapter concludes this eBook. Finally, if you enjoyed this book, please take the time to share your thoughts and post a review on Amazon. It'd be greatly appreciated! Thank you, good luck and happy gifting!

BONUS: Gifts in Jars You Could Easily Make

Some people wonder: Why, on earth, would you wish to make your own gifts in jars? But it is so easy to tell the reason – in fact, many reasons.

- **Think of the cost.**

If you picked some ornament that you bought years ago on impulse and to-date have never found a place to hang or even display it, would it not be like hitting two birds with the same stone? You would be saving your house clutter and pleasing someone else at the same time, and that, at no cost whatsoever.

The same case applies if you have some nice gifts that have outlived their usefulness. For example, you could have some religious items that were given to you once when you were a church leader, and you have since, for some personal reasons, turned atheist. Would you not love to oblige someone else who is still walking in the straight and narrow with such religious gifts? You would only need to pack them nicely in a jar, write a few kind words, and you have some nice package to give a friend.

- **Think of relevance**

You see, packing your own gifts is very different from buying ready-made because when you are doing it, you just include gift items you are confident your recipient will be excited about.

For example, when buying gifts in jars, chances are you could realize that the jar that is close to what you want has two great items for your purpose, say, a bar of chocolate and a can of fresh juice, but then inside there you find some sachets of brandy. Surely, is that a jar of gifts you want to buy your adolescent niece? But you do not encounter such problems when you are preparing the gifts in jars yourself.

- **Think of convenience**

What on earth can hinder you from packing one nice set of acrylic nails and a set of hair clips together with some tubes of lip gloss, all in one jar; then tie a beautifully colored ribbon round the gift jar and give it to someone as a gift? Yet this is something you can do at a moment's notice when you have all these items in your house.

- **Think of Creativity**

Hey! Gifts are not necessarily about bringing someone above the poverty line. In fact, many of the people you give gifts to are self sufficient without your little token. Still, you get a chance to test how creative you can be. Who says you cannot bake cookies in baby faces and see how some kids react to them? Or candies in pencil shapes? In fact, your creativity testing could even manifest in the way you arrange the different gifts in a jar.

Examples of DIY Gifts in Jars

1) Baileys and chocolate

Say you get yourself some container and fill it halfway with hot chocolate and marshmallows. Then close it and put it inside your gift jar. Then you take a bottle of Baileys and put it in the same gift jar which you then seal.

What do you think is going to happen when your gift reaches its destination? For me, I see excitement and celebratory mood. Exposing the Baileys content and pouring some inside the container with hot chocolate and marshmallow creates a beverage that can spoil you to hell; well, the not-so-evil brand of hell. All this shows you how easy it is to compile a unique set of gifts in a jar; a gift that the recipient cannot forget for a long time to come.

2) Assortment of food classes in a jar

Talk of energy and you have it in your jar of gifts. Speak of refreshments and you have them. Then there are those niceties that you put in just as spoils.

The energy gifts in the jar could include peanuts; a chocolate mix; some latte mix; some nut energy bar; and possibly some chocolate truffles.

The refreshments could include any drink you can think of, like cola, fresh juice and such. When it comes to pampering goodies, you could include any kind of lotion; small face towels; disposable toothbrushes; and so on.

3) Items to detox

Imagine opening a gift jar and finding a range of items which you can use to detoxify your body! If you acknowledge you would be excited, especially knowing how much of dirty stuff we take in through inhaling; touching; and also ingesting; you will appreciate that such items would be welcome to other people too as gifts.

Some detoxifying items you can include in your jar of gifts are daily cleansers; peeling gel; detox tea; and so on.

4) Some Honey Butter mix

Surely you can mix honey and butter and mash them into a nice and even mix. When, on top of that you season that mixture with cinnamon, you find yourself with a unique tasting mix that you can use on baked products and other food items as well.

Just remember to decorate your gift jar with beautiful, albeit simple, ribbons. That will complement the uniqueness of the product to make the gift recipient feel special.

5) Sports Team Wear

Suppose you have a friend who is crazy about a particular sports team. Can you not make a great gift by packing some arm band with the team's name; a well folded hood with the team's name; and any other tiny item with the team logo or name on it?

And this is where you need to be up to date with your friend's tastes. You had better be certain your friend is still with the team you are dealing with. You do not want to send gifts in a jar screaming we are Team A till death do us part only to find the guy has long ditched that team for Team B that possibly does not see eye to eye with Team A.

6) A jar of wallet, phone case and key holder

These are items you can pack well in a jar of gifts and present as a personalized gift. If, for example, your recipient is fascinated by crocodiles, you could select items that are made of crocodile leather and provide a pleasant surprise.

7) Pancakes, eggs and milk in a Jar

When you are on a DIY program, you have a wide range of choice when it comes to pancakes. You could try out cinnamon seasoned pancakes; or a different flavor. In your jars of gifts, you could also pack some small packets or cans of fresh milk, and some boiled eggs. How handy such jars of gifts can be to someone going out with kids, say, for a picnic or a short trip away from the city eateries and hotels!

8) Cowboy cookies and refreshment

With rich crunchy cowboy cookies in your jar of gifts, you could also add some packets of fresh juice or blend some and pack in small bottles. If you want to be a little more experimental, possibly you may try mixing your own vodka and honey and packing it nicely. This will be a welcome gift for anyone who travels or anyone who likes taking it easy on the balcony on a sunny weekend.

Printed in Great Britain
by Amazon